BASSINET

Books by Dan Rosenberg

Poetry
A Thread of Hands
The Crushing Organ
cadabra
Thigh's Hollow

Translation
Hippodrome by Miklavž Komelj, with Boris Gregoric

BASSINET

DAN ROSENBERG

Carnegie Mellon University Press
Pittsburgh 2022

Acknowledgments

Many thanks to the editors of the following journals, who published these poems in these or earlier versions:

The Academy of American Poets' Poem-a-Day: "Order"
The Adroit Journal: "What Will Survive"
Alaska Quarterly Review: "Handprints on a Paper Lantern"
Beecher's: "Fissure"
Better: Culture & Lit: "Grown-up Love"
Blackbird: "Spacemen Specimen"
Conjunctions: "Buttermilk Falls," "Field Guide," "Serval," "Splitting the Worm," "To Wake from a Crowded Dream Alone"
jubilat: "Best Friends"
Leveler: "Prayer"
Mid-American Review: "If You Carry the Book I Will Carry You"
The New York Quarterly: "Filling the Lake"
North American Review: "Bassinet," "Husbandry," "Sliding House"
Pangyrus: "My Rabid Boy"
Ploughshares: "The Gnat and the Lion, January 2017"
Poet Lore: "On Worship"
Stone Canoe: "To Miles, January 2015"
Unstuck: "The Golem," "Sea Oats"
Verse: "Bonehouse," "Brisk," "Caught in the Car Seat," "Cause and Effect," "Dear B.," "A Fifth Question," "Forever in an Ice Cream Truck," "Homeopathy," "Independent Love I," "Is It Astronomy or Astrology," "Memento Merry," "Mine," "Musician Courting," "Paces," "Riding the Clutch," "To My Wife's Good Ear," "What Mooring," "Wish You Were Here," "Your Old Home Is a Destination Now."

Thank you as well to the editors of these publications for including my work:

A Constellation of Kisses (Terrapin Books 2019): "Cause and Effect"
From the Finger Lakes: A Memoir Anthology (Cayuga Lake Books 2021): "Husbandry," "Buttermilk Falls"
From the Finger Lakes: A Poetry Anthology (Cayuga Lake Books 2016): "Best Friends"
Likovne besede (*Artwords*): "A Fifth Question," in Miklavž Komelj's Slovene translation as "Peto Vprašanje"
Till the Tide (Sundress Publications 2015): "Sea Oats"

"To Miles, January 2015" was printed as a broadside by Richard Kegler at Wells College Press.

Book design by Trevor Lazar

Library of Congress Control Number 2021946632
ISBN 978-0-88748-676-0

10 9 8 7 6 5 4 3 2 1

Thou, sun, art half as happy as we,
In that the world's contracted thus.

—John Donne

Contents

IV ❧ Haunt

V ❧ Field Guide

I ◆ To Bear

Husbandry

The green beans topple
on thin stems. Two rats

pack their peas across the skin
of last night's rain. Again

I have tied the wild
to a stake and bid it grow.

A sparrow, flush with seeds,
stuck headfirst in the feeder,

eats and freaks and eats
until I reach up, tug it

by the tail feathers.
It weighs nothing like

a heartbeat. Like a breath,
I release it into the magnolia,

press my heels back down
to the grass. Below, a world

thrums in the dirt, sheared
bricks and landlocked sea glass

the worms weave through,
smoothed slowly with each

step and root. Still deeper,
the dead spill their heat

from here to the horizon.
They don't rise. What rises

rises from them while I stand
planted here and sinking.

Musician Courting

For the deep draws of your song
have I come to hunger in this drizzle.
Outside your window, panting
at the sill. Above, the moon

bears its footprints into the dark,
but I'm caught about the ears still
by the bright music you once made.
I can see my breath upon the pane,

its wet meander, as if the air itself,
transformed inside my lungs, could
also feel the phantom song clenched
tight as pain at the edge of my ear.

You sang of red sand, of apricots
dried along a clay roof; you sang
of spider venom milked into a cup.
What I heard was pulse, beaten breath,

a tracing of blood to its drum source.
You promised the well's clean foundation,
dry stone beneath my head.
In your song I heard the adder

hush itself across the dirt, dignified
as a spill of acorns, and here I am
in the short grass, ears cocked.
Against my cheek your house lows

and cups the earth. You sang once
of its slow decline, or at least I heard
it decline once, and you were singing,
and each star locked into place,

and the ash tree shed its branches
to better point at the sky.

Serval

Our bed is elevated. The serval hunts
on wires. Breaks open a butterfly. Dust
crushed in a vertical pounce. Lovemaking

on the proscenium. And lovemaking
in the hardware section. Our bed,
strung on wires. Our serval makes

a proscenium of love. We break
open the butterfly with a vertical
crush. Our eyes closed in deep grass

for up to fifteen minutes, the stillness
before the leap. Your paws clamp down.
Break open our lovemaking: the dust

crushes out. What else so honestly
powders itself to our paws? Butterflies,
hunted. Make do with the wares

we have offered each other. We receive
a proscenium closed in deep grass.
Your serval breaks open her hardware,

dusts our bed. And at my pounce
a proscenium closes. Your paws clamp
our bed: a lovemaking. The hunter

sleeps a hunt in our bed. The feline
twitch and flex of hardware. We elevate
our hands, the bed, we hunt the butterfly,

a vertical pounce. This lovemaking
breaks open. What dust crushes out
from us. What dust on wires we are.

What dust so honestly itself in deep grass
for up to fifteen minutes. The eyes clamp
on wires. The butterfly, dust-hunting.

The proscenium closes our lovemaking.
What else on wires, what else breaks
open: the hunter the hunted loves making.

Bassinet

We meet the afternoon half dressed. The umbrella hangs darkly, curled from a cord. Then the downpour and us: all parched and short memory. You tell me to bring my innards to bear, but the catch won't catch; our windows blink and streak. Our time doesn't recognize itself in the weather. Now we can't tell who's crying, in what language. A smoke break takes the wind. We hold our lungs in our hands.

*

The fish are microscopic, each half a person in the orange light. To survive, we direct them into each other. Keep the gods busy splitting thunder. That way we can sneak under the dogwoods in the dimly lit park. The hedge celebrates its shearing, but the grass would rather not be put upon. We don't hear with our hearts. What sneaks past is a ball, then a cluster of balls. The gods drown and drown us. Nothing more alone than a peeled can of sardines. Two drunk wine tasters in a corner booth. I touch your belly; just your belly touches back.

*

Pursuant to the weather we have found each other wholly. We thread our hand-me-down hearts. We fold our hearts and make the incisions. They accordion out, patron saints of a party we keep throwing for ourselves. Two goldfish in a glass bowl exhaust each other. We take turns making noises with our mouths. The third chair braces itself unnecessarily.

*

Her juggling has gone awry somewhere below the intestines, she says. The candle is stuttering and drooling to the floorboards. The house grows thin. We can see its veins; we can see its vacant ducts. The door is a scar. She steps through her scar to show it can be done, but nobody does.

A Fifth Question

for Tomaž Šalamun

And what now the lighthouse is blind.
The stars bump into each other,
miss their careful, accidental balance.
And what now the turtles are without their braids.
You said they were immoral but I thought
you said immortal. They spilled from you
like any one was too frail to survive
on its own, like rabbits, like the shadows
of imaginary rabbits on the bedroom wall.
The ocean is parched, the moonlight heavy.
When it rains the angels are not sad. You said
the angels are never sad. It's just rain on my face.
I am looking up. And what now you're not
in Ljubljana. What now am I to say to the earth
when it whispers in your voice. The sparrows
will not merge. The third tree bows to her mountain.
Look at her exuberant leaves pretending
to be the sky from below, pretending
to be the grass from above. Riddled with
sparrows. Look at the mountain
sitting his way into the diamond business.
And what now you are like rocks
done with getting older. And what now
the semaphores are calling after you.
It looks like a dance but the flags are not touching.
Look at everyone's empty hands.

Fissure

Now the earth gives up
its shrugging mid-meadow,

> lets the boots have their way.
> Over flatness, the beetle lumbers

in an imperative of shade,
the space between stars on its back.

> The cat's eyes, smudged with milk.
> The kill has left him,

splayed like a bramble.
With old claws curling back.

> And me? I'm carried in scars.
> Once a fall was how

the story started. The baby
listing from chair to chair,

> the wobble. Light dripping
> from a joyous mouth.

The earth was the sun once. Now
boots trample and we bear it.

> Bear the mark: the path carves the land.
> Deer are baffled. The asphalt swath.

The moon got a new crater
and nobody cried. Our flags up there

are mostly bleached out by now.
And me? What would break a rock

must be harder than the rock.
Or it can find the fissure.

Cause and Effect

after Dean Young

Because we are so thoughtless
we kiss each other on the holes

we speak from, we cross our legs
upon each other, angling in,

always angling in. The fireplace
is electric, but that doesn't stop

our melding on the hardwood.
Because we are so hungry we stare

like owls at the bar-lit faces
of strangers we know

we're supposed to want.
You are a deep-sea diver

and I'm an inactive volcano.
You are a starfish and I'm

a rash from a wetsuit. You are
four honeymooners and I'm

the blonde walking by.
Because we are so close

our fingertips catch. You plunge us
into the ocean. I speak in bubbles.

You grow a shell and I'm the grit
in your mantle. We irritate

each other. We produce a pearl.

Sea Oats

I soaked my oats. I soaked a merman
out of my oats. He must have been
dehydrated, disintegrated, vacuum-sealed.
With a honeyed finger I touched
his flesh. He purred. A thread of light
knotted my fingertip. A hummingbird
struck my window red. At my screen door
a pale deer chewed out her own heart.
In a kitchen like this, I couldn't tell
if I was sweating or if the ants had come
to crown me in a drippy swarm.
Never had my home pulsed so,
the Cuisinart sparking as the walls
stuttered through their dance. I took
a fork to the merman's hair, took
it to my mouth. I could hear the squirrels
thrashing in the ventilation. To slurp
a merman from his pot, what finer
pleasure is there? He tasted
like a wafer, but to think of him
as a thing to be tasted was disgraceful.
I welcomed him carefully, my body
a jangle of parts rough hewn.
I couldn't tell with my tongue
the divide between torso and tail:
He came to me as one wholesome form,
a cloud whipped into tornado.
I felt the foundation shift, heard
from inside myself the ecstatic
sound of teeth realizing the foam.

Homeopathy

From the pathogen fields,
the bronchial reservoir scrum
and its miasma, and its unguents,
you are hacking forth, poor B.,
battered about your innards
and sopped in tea stain and spice.
Again I'll fetch the cough drop,
again the raw honey congealed
in its glass jar, some benevolent mucus
meant to contradict the phlegm
you're full of. But enough.
Wasteland body I love, enough.
I'll be your balance, yes, and fill
each mug I find around the house
with water. Cracked seed, visible web.
Unused gym bag behind the shoes.
I'll be the crook of your elbow,
kiss this sickness from you.

The Golem

has come to your
neighborhood.
The golem
scratches the letters
on his head. He has
the fist of nails.
He scrapes
accidental trenches
in himself.
His gloves
have blood
of their own.
His foot
snaps your azaleas:
a freezing sound.
Pie smells
turn to burnt
smells. There is
trembling.
The golem
will not kill anyone
for you, will not
tie a rope
between man
and child's body.
Where are your dead?
Where did you get
these bodies?
The golem
will let them rot.
His head tilts back.
There is no
Adam's apple,

his face does not
crack in the sun.
You want to give
him a book. You
want to touch
his cheek. Don't.
The golem is
clay baked
and coughed into.

Birth Plan

It starts inside my left ear, an itch,
a tick biting into being its own
bullseye, legs flailing in joy,
in joy or primal need sated.
Somehow, it pierces me.

Incubates. It drifts in red fog
behind my brow, finds the blister
on my palm, drops a tendril in.
It sips the bone and grows

and grows like an ecosystem,
a covenant. It tweaks my knee
when I stand by the birthing tub.
With its noose of light, it pinches
off a corner of my lungs. My steps

grow foxlike in the hospital.
I learn to whisper through
a cowl. When I finally sleep,
I push an invisible stroller

up the walls. Stones and stones
in bonnets fall, batter my arms
until they're red and tender.
I wake in rubble, touch
my wife's wet knee. From deep

in the sea she's made herself
she turns to me, no, through me,
toward the waiting room, where
my father is breathing into balloons.

II ◆ Mine

My Rabid Boy

after Yehuda Amichai

My rabid boy: Each evening
he thrashes my fancy, catches
my every idea in his teeth.
He tears them. I am his woodland.
I feel him sharpen his claws
on my heart. I hear
his mews and snarls circle
each hair on my neck.

My rabid boy, my tarantula
stitching a nest of my hunger,
shushing my efforts at speech.
I crawl inside him.

I want to cock my ears
behind his ears,
like how under a cloud the owl
freezes, gathers herself,
and dives to transmute a vole.

Brisk

The window has squared the landscape
or will, tomorrow, when our son
bails himself from sleep and finds
you, zonked, sprawled and topless,
and me, eyelids like gristle, desperate
for a few quiet minutes more. My heart
is a rooster, B. Its beak is buried
in its breast. It rests but fitfully, knowing
in some terse infantile way the coyote
is just past the corner, breathing
visibly on the chilled pane.

Riding the Clutch

I write this late morning from behind
and behind the steering wheel
while our snot muffin snores
in the back. Having made it
here we wait, twin hermit crabs
pinching the air awhile.

The sky looks like the bottom
of a tea kettle, and we are dripped
upon, some kind of confirmation.
From here I can see cars going
and going away. The clouds
are in a rush too, but seem to be
barely untethered from the still ground.

To Miles, January 2015

You burnish my residue, little man,
partially formed & incapable of lying.

When I think I can't be chewed
anymore you are on my arm,

head whipping like a kill-shake,
a deranged and gummy harmonica solo.

Concave mirror, dirty bundle of need,
but I am full as the world of need

for you. Full as fire. You wear me
to the wick & I keep dancing.

For you I turn the record, snap
the straps, harness you to my chest.

I groove my path around the room for you.
I strengthen my back & bear & bear.

Forever in an Ice Cream Truck

Forever in an ice cream truck
wouldn't be so bad, wheeling
my way around the neighborhood
with one long song dragging
behind me like a wake. The kids

tumbling toward not where I am
but where they know I'll be. The sun
lazing about the sky in a slow
circle, never setting, just spinning
our shadows around us. And you

would have to be there too, alive
to the repetitive joys of summer.
If I had my hand on the wheel,
I'd drive the world and you
past breaking, to the sticking point.

Dear B.

Half a bottle of Pinot Noir
and I know I'm funny. Home
at last I'm thick about the brain
and thirstified. Dear B.,
I've eaten the artichoke,
its sharp leaves, its tender heart.
But here my feeding is outward.
I feed my arm under our son,
his head a hot compress on my veins.
I feed this grown-man ego,
calling another human *mine*.
What is this having if not a self
expanding? And I was out drinking
without you. Our son is a son
of fire. Our son I fear is a son
drowning in the eye of small fame.
It is deep and cold. It is a pool
we are building together. I don't
imagine a world without him
tonight. Tonight I am happy
and drunk. The pillow here
is my body. Together, we three are
giddy as vapors. Stern as stones.

Bonehouse

Why does this woman you're watching
want so little of the world? Did she learn
at last that some people are different

from other people? B., your pleasures
sometimes disgust me. But here I burrow
into your sternum anyway. It is comfortable

as a bed of keys. I play a game
on my phone: The aliens must be
eliminated, and I have the blaster.

Beneath my ear something inside you
unlocks. I can listen, I think, to this
terrible movie, and save the universe,

and hear this body beneath me, its
slow, necessary unwinding. The woman
suddenly loves her friend and runs

in a hot panic from her career.
I'm wrapping myself around you,
a listless barnacle on a listless hull.

Caught in the Car Seat

We've raised a world around a person.

We grow old like the sea inside him.

We are always loud; we are always moving.

Water breathes in the ferns.

Water sucks the sand and we totter.

Our son wakes up somewhere new to him.

Don't take from the cat his unnecessary claws.

The cup won't let go of its old milk.

The smell is attractive to something unlike us.

The grass is not green, but greens.

Our son suddenly knows what we're saying.

Or can suddenly show us the old fact.

We're busy ordering the world.

From where he sits the world recedes.

What Mooring

Bitter rose, banded rose, the thumb flesh quickly pierced. I feel the violation first as pressure, then the pain, then the bleed. I'm holding my hand in my hand, in the pollen's visible orbit. Briar heart, numb fawn, you put elastic around the dimmer stars and snapped. Now we've lost our north. Now the fireman sits under his ladder watching the sky fail. Night strapped down, straining Pleiades. Now the moth flame remembers the color of honey. The table collects my thumbprints, speckled as the heavens. The table fields no time, no turn.

Is It Astronomy or Astrology

Tired as old honey I've sunk my faith
and fortune to the footwell and slumped,
head on the wheel as if by thinking
I could change direction. As if the stars

were steadfast in the sky, worth driving by.
Bright wife, I snipe and rake. I silence, smart-ass,
I know. The hippie preacher yesterday
said to be ourselves, but I want for you

a better man than me. Here is the limit
of my good husbandry: He's asleep
in the car seat. And I'll park here and breathe,
bring my little corner of our world back

to right angle, and when our son stirs
I'll call him softly into his body,
serve him like a map to a better map,
to manhood more complete, to you.

Our small nebula, our wet penny moaning
his way back to the car now, to me, staying,
waiting for him, so we can leave
the parking lot and totter up to you.

Grown-up Love

Inside the sacrament our child lies
and ages and three kinds of hunger sag

over the belt of his being ours. Such a
child we have in the shared spaces,
such a boulder comes tumbling, picks up

pine cones, permissions, his face grows angled
and sun-touched, our cranial mush, yeah, we'd give
for him, the mortality clause, the sun

a cheap orange we tear with our nails.
And we look to feed, and we feed to love.
And when he eats he eats us alive.

And when he's done we sweep ourselves
together, the dribble of us, we cake to his toes,
to his heels' downturn, a thin layer,

leftover, hoping to soften one
or two steps on the ungiving ground.

Wish You Were Here

We see three birds squabbling between the two
gray-green pines. A cloud arranged like a slow
brain. The moon, though it is daytime, and the erratic
breeze mumbles warmly. A green tanker truck, its engine
guttural and unforgiving, dopplers by,
then is lost to water, its kind erasure.
A line of five apple trees, filtering
the sunlight. The faintest glimmer of my white
forehead, and his whiter one, pressed
against the windowpane like spectators
or specters eavesdropping on the mortal world.

To My Wife's Good Ear

The flaxseed etches your gums.
You have to bite it
if you want to break it down.

The good lord picks up rocks
and wants to bite them. I snatch
each rock from his mouth.

I am a high priest of something.
You are in between mythologies
like a swan or a dead battery.

To power the world, we feed.
To power the world we feed,
we feed him some more.

You have to slice the avocado
like a circumnavigator, twist it
open until its stone is visible,

nested like a star. And he
will call it a ball and not be wrong.
What keeps us going is this

familiar routine, the small strainer
is just for peas, apples for horses,
carrots for horses, but horses

themselves a kind of cracker
we keep coming. If you eat,
you become. My throat is scarred

with food I couldn't use as food.
It affects my singing.
It makes my singing better.

I'll Take It

You drag us into ourselves you
mix of us jolting wonkily forth
under this summer burden of sky
this heavy sky not fallow
but sterile in heat sloth you
tick the day before the day's
heat has begun its slow slow
penetration a ringmaster of plush
you array the circus between us
but I am here missing some ways
to explain this joy burden
as the sky heaves down light
to our corner of planet and yes
each bush each scrub seems
at first grateful under the burn
but wilts to wan like Sappho
says not envy but hunger and here
with too many pens in my pocket
what I'm saying is the sun frightens
dark spots into my skin this
thing meant to nourish to nurture
can burn us animals the plants know
like you no restraint they thrust forward
to a world that will or will not hold
and yes there is in the leap glory
and glory in the fall but when
you fall my heavy blood pump
catches I feel it where only I'm
supposed to be and here you are
small reckless thunder you fall
out of our bed our little world
its center its walls its sphere shake
with the impact though carpeted

though you cry our world awake
it is too early I am too old for this
too much life too much I'll take it

III ◆ Buckle

Handprints on a Paper Lantern

What's in the sky? *Airplanes, rockets,*
the moon, he says. A finished list.

He answers for always, not for now.
His shoes illuminate the ground.

The moon is there, yes, I say,
but the sun's too busy to let us see it.

He's like rogue mint, unafraid of weather.
Learning the world through its cracks.

Just do what water does, I say,
reaching for something inside him.

He sees no birdseed left in the brown
clay bowl. What else gets hungry, I say.

The clouds draw their curtain. *An eye,*
he says. It's closed, I say. *Open it,* he says.

Order

I hear you wake before I'm up myself
and snap to ready now before my eyes
crack from their crud to face your face today.
I hear you blunder toward my door. I hear

you crash it wide. The loosened hinges shiver
their frame, and now the house itself, awake
to the world and you, complicit, pulls me hard
as thunder from my sleep. You beat the echoes

to me, blear faced, awash with night sweat;
you drag a bunny by the ears to bed
and tumble graceless up the mattress, silent,
a drowsy rocket wanting, wanting something

I'm not awake enough to understand
but will be, soon, my son, and then we'll go
to blaze the day, to stomp each puddle left
by the rain you never notice as you pull

me into the world, all leap and bowl, all grab
and fall. Today I'll wake up better, call
the distance order, order it to be
a smaller thing. I'll stand to make it so.

Paces

Wobbling in the parking lot,
heel to toe to heel our son then

shot forth like a purebred foal
on a tangent to our home.
I had in me no thought
of not following. Fathering

by brute repetition I measured
out the invisible leash strung
from his nape to my ribs. As he
teetered on the cusp of the lawn

I felt the tug deep in my chest,
the anchor seat of polished oak
throbbing its imaginary wounds
at every raw, uncomprehending cry.

But he had today no fear or falls,
no honest contact
with the world's rough edges.

Only another turn, inscrutable
as a butterfly's, and he was straddling
the asphalt and the sidewalk,

his small right foot a half foot
higher than his left. And walking
like that, he reached a confident hand

up behind him, eyes relentlessly
undressing the path ahead, and there

of course was my hand. He curled
his fingers on my index finger.

I sheathed his hand in mine up to the wrist.
He was thinking of the world to hurl
himself, from me, into. I was thinking of
the world he's worried into me.

If You Carry the Book I Will Carry You

A train thrown from its tracks can be forgotten
if the grass grows tall enough or the observer
is sufficiently small.

The wind doesn't mind
the maple leaves grown frantic
about its presence.

Just so,
beside the busted window AC unit,
I don't mind the mule in the mirror.

Just because
it's got four wheels doesn't make it
a car, I've never said

to our son, for whom one
wooden block is a battery, another
the face of a locomotive.

Perfectly framed in the window,
he watches the world
unfold around his brief stillness.

We'll empty all our stuff
from the two-door Honda
in three smart trips

or, more likely, one precarious one.
Here is home for now
with its circles of light.

Telephone poles drip rain,
tell us nothing
but the weather.

Memento Merry

In the picture you're holding
a bird skull it is dry white and empty
its weight almost imperceptible
almost the beak pressed quietly
into a crease in your hand it may be
your life line but is certainly
where the flesh folds when you hold
an object in your hand a bird skull
smaller than your thumb tip you are
holding it out now and my camera
has focused on it thoughtlessly
blurring in the grass behind you
our son failing to blow bubbles

Your Old Home Is a Destination Now

So. Having stopped for avocados
every other hour we've arrived
at your parents' house. The backyard lake
bucks and stretches its film. Geese do nothing

in the neighbor's lawn. Our son bolts
toward all, each step a brief release of the wild
these two days in the car have wound tight
inside him. And me? I still stumble, grin,

perform the father with honest joy and honest
sleepiness. Our son reaches up
for his grandma's hand and lunges toward the steps.
I see you twinge from your core as if to leap

at them, to save each from the other. But we
came here for the opposite, to cement
for our son where he's fallen from, to gift
your parents this precipice, this overreach.

Splitting the Worm

We scuttle to a stop at the lake edge,
at the fat plop of a frog's retreat

we always barely fail to see. Here
we're ankled in spawn grown bolder:

earth crumbling aside instead of down,
each chunk of dirt legged and speckled.

And now unsteadied by this ground
gone pulsing we freeze at the thought:

What creatures have we trampled
in our careless tumble to the water?

Three geese skim by, unconvinced.
A buck regrets us. And these rejections

are just the ones we see. What blistered
systoles we impose with each heel

pressed down on the underworld.
The blind worms suffer our weight,

scorn the light. An arrowhead of sear
on my arm, a divot of flesh in my wrist,

and here the mosquitoes learn nothing
from my flailing. I try to understand

the world's single body here in the scrum
of the shore. Something surfaces

as if from a mirror, and I don't recognize it.
B., even here, I can't deny

my separateness. Sink, love, less than half
of our shared flesh, into the lake that raised

you. Submerge to your roots. I'll stay here,
sceptic lighthouse, itchy at the border.

Raleigh, Christmas

Being the bigger parent with a voice
angled toward command I have less

trouble wrangling him than my wife
who sees in each squirrel and each

hydrangea a possible conversation.
Here before the phony evergreen

bedazzled with chintz he leans, eyes
nailed to my seeing him, into the draw

of his presents. Some parental test:
his watching me watch him

while his mother manages her own.
And as the afternoon falls over,

the laughing inches closer to tears.
I scoop him from the misshapen star

ornament his mother made when she
was him. I lumber through a house

bedecked with Christmas traditions,
a halfhearted Jew rooting his son

in the unfamiliar love I find
here among these artifacts

of nobody's actual faith, his mother's
world of memory and order. Our son

at least wants his world upended,
and a clementine, and so I take him

by the ankles, spin him around
so he can see the world around him spin.

Prayer

All twisted up in his mother's pouch,
the joey seems unaccountably
comfortable. Clouds cut a mountain range,

jagged the sky. There's a peacock
tangled in the hedgerow. *No cars*

remember the bridge when they leave,
I say. But the dust in the air hangs

around each *thump* like a bee swarm
circling its queen. We breathe it. My son
requests a fourth story: the kangaroo

bounds into its next life, or what
the shrubs know. *Some hotdog vendors*
are royal; some finches are loyal, I say.

I tell him the dandelions are moon-
flowers. Turns out there are many

real moonflowers, none so intricate
and common. I love the winter

for showing the thick air we share.
How like our minds are the reef fish,

nestled in the coral. How deep
the light, stripping itself away,
descends. Below, some breathers

muck the currents. I am not stingy
with my exhales. Son, ambergris
starts disgusting but sweetens.

Filling the Lake

My pine cone pricks
my fingers on the windup,
wobbles overhead,
plops through
the water's false sky.

My son's tumbles
limp from shore to shallows,
and he crows
and crows. The sky
distills its cool,

and we—upright
on flattened grass—
don't think overmuch
on the weather, time:
just bluster and be
on the edge.

His winter
coat zipper keeps
bursting its middle.
I align the teeth,
pull hard as heaven
against his growth.

Sliding House

Dear empathy, you're far away
but mostly we're willing to push

the revolving door a touch harder
for whoever comes after, and I don't believe

in underlying order, no faint meridians parallel
as pipes, shoving the eye neatly around.

There is no *neatly* in the summation
of forces that turn us, no gesture that says

more of this done perfectly until the world
is complete. Slow waves, be slow.

Worn sky, conceal us.
When each tangled wave thinks itself

a circle, we arc around an empty center.

Weeding

I shove through bush and bed,
stumping along our house. Somewhere
I learned not to let the plants grow
too close, something about air flow, rot,

our home's slow demolition by vine.
I wrap my hand around a dandelion,
pull into the tension, breathless
for the slight snap of roots, then harder,

until the earth releases it, or it gives up
its hold on the ground. I sunder
something deep, throw the plant
with its knot of dirt

to the driveway. The foliage
extends. A branch slaps back,
leaves an archipelago of blood
along my calf. Another, another,

I don't know their names, just
pull with faith in the prior owner,
in her fertile excess that even my blunders
won't undo. One white twig

feels hollow, comes loose in my hand,
but what of it was underground is red
as a crime, bent and beckoning.
The spring's first accidental sweat

catches in the corners of my squint.
When I stand upright, survey
my labor, nothing looks better.

Independent Love I

But enough trios,
enough dancing between

you and me
and this child

made of us.
I write tonight

to you, wife,
independent love I

hold dear to
my breast like

a rusted windlass.
What we lift

we lift together.
You back up

into my crotch
in the kitchen

like a cobra,
all hiss and

slither, dangerous and
cold. You ask

if your dress
shines. I have

nothing to say
but what bears

repeating: Yes, yes.

IV ◈ Haunt

What Will Survive

This small gray stone nestled
between two larger speckled ones,

maybe. Some crickets, but not
this one. The mountain, as silt,
as ocean floor. What trash

we've launched into the cold
between worlds. The word

sedimentary will not. Nor this
heat between us. The twinge
in my hip, the crook of your grin,

every murmured word
in the predawn blear of being

together, no. But maybe
for a while the scar our son
carries like a secret kiss

in the new valley of his back.
Which won't survive even

as long as the brick he buried
between our yard and the woods
when spring called him to the dirt

again. That foolhardy seed.
Maybe not the pleasure

of fingers digging down,
but the dirt itself, the good
or unclean dirt. The ribs at least

of the city where we live.
Some atoms shaking

in the air between us now,
surely, but not the knowledge
that now they are here, here.

This metal closet handle,
torn loose. How the ocean

erases what's marked on the shore.
The desire of anything to tilt
its head when watching a puddle's

surface, to right what it is
we see reflected there.

The Gnat and the Lion, January 2017

Some gnats live on the land and some on the water.
Many eat plants and some are carnivores.
They are everywhere people are; they live
on subantarctic islands, in deserts, caves.
When they fly they're usually so numerous
they look like weather. The weather at dusk.
Some are pests and some control pests.
Some don't bite and die quickly.
Some love mushrooms. Others, not so much.
They are no larger than a few grains of salt.
The main sign of gnats is that you see them.
Some are attracted to wet eyes.
After a prolonged wet period, they will appear.
They will appear under every streetlight.
Some appear in such numbers they block the light.
They live in meadows, forests, swamps.
To control them, don't expose your fruits.
They thrive on your fruits but also
what's dying around you, or thriving too much.
Some gall plants for food and shelter.
Some are at least partly predatory.
Some can glow as children but not adults.
Some adults can glow which makes them
both lure for prey and target for predators.
You may find this beautiful or not.
"You strain out a gnat and swallow a camel."
We don't know how many there are,
how many shapes and colors and sizes.
Several kinds of females are wingless.
They're small. We know they're small.
They reproduce in ghosts.

To Wake from a Crowded Dream Alone

is sweeter than the bee's
delicate legs, sweeter
than paper, than the maple
weeping through the coattails
of winter.

      I wake
to the house wren's staccato
song: He wants a mate,
drab little bird, so he
sings a promise of home
mostly to the wrong
audience: me. He cracks
the shell of sleep as if
the world were daily hatched.
And I declare to the wall
his desperate, lonely song
is sweet.

      Sweet as my son
panting into a globe
of dandelion seeds, believing
his regular breath
can set them to flight.
He holds tight the wonder
of tiny feathers drifting
away from his lips,
the sudden transformation
to unremarkable stump
and stem in his fist.
He's bright-eyed and thoughtless
of where the seeds will fall
and what will grow there.

But now he is elsewhere,
the wren is past the window,
I've scraped the pulp
of sleep from my eyes,
and it is spring. The light
passes through each new-torn
leaf. The bearded irises
look sexual and alien.
They huddle together,
sprouts of forgotten bulbs.

They don't remind us
of us, their heads
devout with color, jostled
indirectly toward the sun.
What remind us of us
are the thin holes in the skin
of the day, separating
each thread of grass,
each twig just a twig,
not yet part of a nest.

From the space inside
each iris, the stamen
lifts its grains of pollen,
their solitude and potential
unconsidered, and when
the bee translates them
to a neighbor, this meeting
is an accident. So familiar,
this being brought together
by something else's hunger.

Best Friends

I'll give you my hair if you give me your skull.
I'll give you my feet if you give me your wheels.
I'll give you your face if you give me mine again.
What's owned in the world between us anyway.
A stomach that's been punched for your hunger.
My equanimity for just one fist flowering into hand.
Just one, friend. I'll open my eyes if you open.
I'll stay beside you if you. I'm unsexed and you
are the font of hunger. Your breast keeps time
with my breathing. Let's go to a show and you've
already seen it. Let's watch old movies and you're
a bristle cocked for adventure. You're a flea circus
and I'm a metal comb. I'm a rusty trampoline
and you're three small children. I'll play in you
if you play in me, the beloved. We'll never leave
the odd one out. In the dim exterior of love
we'll never leave him. You know the cold and I
know the cold, friend. I'll give you my blood
if you give me your blood. We can circulate
the blood between us. We will live forever, you and I.
Like stars we'll live. I'll orbit you if you orbit me.
Have my ears, I'll hear with your tongue.
I'll shine on you if you glow back at me.
You give me your scars and I'll take them.
Have my hotel room, I'll sleep in your cage.
Friend, turn out the light. Friend, the light.

For Grandma V.

When you died the cardinal
survived, but diminished, fell
into a nuisance. The suction cup
that held its feeder slipped to ruin
on the ground. Your blood was never
spilled like seeds. You faded. Again

this bird returned to nothing. Again
and again you'd press slim cards in all
the grandkids' hands, never
caring which of us shared your blood. You fell
slow as stones through a 96-year-long ruin.
You kept your perfect teeth in a cup.

In your final days, you'd cup
your hand to your ear. *Say that again*,
you'd slur. *We love you*. It's true. In
the youth of love I gave a stuffed cardinal
to my wife. She passed it to our son. It fell
out the open car door. *Some things never*

return to us, I told him. *Never?*
He didn't believe, or understand. He let his cup
drop next, mesmerized as the water fell
along its obvious arc to the pavement. Again
and again, stubborn as you, as the cardinal,
red against your window. True, in

your life were seeds of joy. But mostly rue in
these last lonely years. Never
consoled, you watched Mass on tv. A cardinal
blessed some lady. She drank from a cup
and seemed the same. The sun set again
and rose and you survived. Friends fell

to age, and family, a generation fell
around you like wheat. In your ruined
hands nothing grew again.
Your grand garden I remember never
happened; it was a tiny plot. A cup
of peas at most, three tomatoes, cardinal-

red. You died confused. The paper cup fell
softly from your hand. The cardinal ruined
our shared silence. It will never come again.

On Worship

Our god went amuck, beat
us children with a fist full of seeds.
Our god savored the wind
behind each muffled cry.
When the sun wandered
from the sky our god hid it
poorly. Light leaked from the well.
We called it Showing the Stars.
Our god banished the stars, left
a mirror of black rock in the sky.
The absence it showed
took root in us. The fruit
that grew down from our eyes
into our bowels was all pith,
all rind. Where the flesh wasn't
we felt one whisper that ended
before the next began.
When we made love, our god
was in the bitter taste of peach skin
on each other's lips. When we
bit each other's lips, our god
was audible in the pain. Each
of us named our god anew
over the bodies of our lovers.
We called for blood, like always,
we called for lamb entrails
and daughter flesh. We called
for the sacred mountain
to be peopled. We offered
our god what was multiple
of our bodies. In each meeting
our god sowed a single seed.
We prayed to enter the sacred

mountain, the grove of honeycomb
and village of endless mothers.
Our god, we knew, was taking us
there. The mountain was far,
too far, and that made it sacred.

Provider

Sometimes, friend, a mountain is legible as air,
and sometimes the dust whispers to the crops
its sultry blues—or is it a dirge? Sometimes

it's hard to tell what's a firefly and what's
a forest fire. All you know for sure
is this cricket, how she sidesteps the shovel,

leaping deeper into the darkened garage.
To die, maybe, under a crooked yardstick
notched with years of height. What a future

you try to clever your way into, like a crow
with a pitcher of pebbles. What hot oil freckles
your arms with scars that say *provider*. Cough up

your delicate bones; they won't hold
you upright, and you're no owl deciding
what can be a part of you or not. Sometimes

the laws have loopholes where too many
fingers have worried them away. Or maybe
they were made like that, careless as a lawnmower

shaking a ground wasp nest. Sometimes it's hard
to tell a citrus grove from a circuit board,
but here's the place to sacrifice your son.

Here's a ram, tangled in a bramble. And I'm
over here, finger in nose, holding this ass
by the reins, watching a wide blue nothing stretch

across the sky. Sometimes, friend, you hold
the knife. And sometimes, under a silence of wings
and empty light, the knife just won't be held.

The Stapler

For the hole in the aorta of our nation I've got this stapler.

For the slow descent of the sky I've got this stapler.

For tears pooling in the echo of the dog's sharp bark,

for the poor signal tethering grandpa to grandson

and the absence only one of them knows,

for the buckled sidewalk in front of the food pantry,

for the brown slush in the asparagus bag I've got this stapler.

Good news, democracy. Good news, rhinos. I've got this stapler.

Sometimes in the small blizzard above my desk two papers

will briefly separate, and there is joy. Sometimes even

the wallpaper corners peel out into the room and I know

my stapler isn't what's called for, but it works. It works for now.

I watch the lightning batter the clock tower and I grip my stapler.

I watch the blood moon rise. With it the dead are rising

with no particular desires as if they've exited the elevator

on the wrong floor. My father's father wanders up to me,

working a familiar hat in his bony hands. He spins it slowly.

His mouth is a cave of light. I rise from my desk

and my head is in the blizzard. My eyes go white.

I want to take his hands but I've got this stapler.

Buttermilk Falls

We step on barren stones while between
them the cracks teem with small living.
A game we play: Who can leave the world
most undisturbed. The water says be

like water, leave the slowest fingerprint,
but we can barely hear it over the falls.
The pebbles blunt their edges on our heels.
We are sediment. Two accidental statues,

me and my son, unsteady on the rump of summer.
What counts as life in the slush and wash around us?
The star moss wept somehow against my ankle,

and I seem now more of this place than I was.
Undivorced from stem and root. Untroubled
as a stalagmite under a generous sun. I bend

beside my son, balance stone upon stone.
The moss remains, luminous and still.
We make a home for it, and it survives.

The Rising Path to Cascadilla Falls

purpled thumb-wise
into the evening even
winging it we grew

flightless as a hairdo
do you know   no
love tries to fill the sieve

inverted on your head
your crown a bowl
that couldn't hold a tear

I hear mourning doves
you the garbage truck
we duck under daylight

raise the waterfalls one
bucket at a time   play
knee drums in the gorge

thunder kissing thunder
mists the vision   the creek
mixes its prisms in the air

a breathing violation
unmasks our tenuous grasp
the normal forever reborn

stone torn from the strata
you say *fuck*   project
the *ck*   echo your mama

the water a mirror waves
if I had a smooth hand
if I had solid land
for you

As if They Could Be Caught

when all they want is to ascend
the spider pyramid net climber
and my son is yet unfamiliar
with his body in the world how
to locate his feet his hands
along the ropes but still he rises
taller than me taller than a house
taller than the fence taller than
the Atlantic Ocean taller than a tree
taller than a walrus taller than
a blueberry butt taller than Jasmine
who is five and suspended in air
taller than a hundred taller than
an anthill made of pancakes
taller than a dead bird taller
than the planet Earth this tall
and I am small they say I am so
very small they look down and there
I am far below my small arms out

Spacemen Specimen

On this planet we hadn't yet saddled,
a blanket of craters extended
to a too-near horizon. We had
the just lights of science within us

as we pulled him from the foxhole like an ingrown hair.
He was difficult to see straight, slipping
from our vision's center, but we
were on a mission, full of orders. I remember

the trail his passing left: thick milk
that smelled of pecan pie, of my partner's
first wife's shampoo. We spilled it behind us
as we threaded him from crater to empty crater.

I caught a sense of legs, moving
in unison. He never spoke
in words, and we learned that to hold his arms
was to hold a breach of dust—gently, gently.

We thought we seemed like sun gods to him,
and his trembling some kind of worship.
And the milk dripped from his fingers
as if crushed from foreign stones.

This was after we'd jammed our little flags
into much of the planet, sent our reports
back through an endlessly possible sky.
We did it in triplicate. We were heroes.

Shore

The thick winter sky pivots slowly into dapple. Snow, or the air's long withholding of it, hangs like a promise, unseen. The old men sit and sit on the diminishing benches facing Cayuga Lake, fading down the bike path in their old-world wool caps. Three children scatter a nest of mittens and scarves and coats across the goose-defiled lawn, hurl their overheated bodies toward the shore. Then pause, having gone no farther in their minds than here. A distant cloud or tree branch cracks its knuckle. The men don't move. One girl reaches her hand to the lake, and it seems to reach right back, like always. She recoils inside a squeal of glee, then looks around to nothing: her friends lost in a secret language of pebbles and shards of shell, the men almost floral in their stillness. Slowly, the color in her fingertips shifts toward blue, but she doesn't turn to gather up her clothes. She shivers and then is still. Maybe the lake has reached her. Maybe, in its reaching, she is there. The sky slowly shifts its weight of clouds, marking sudden changes far above.

Hippocampus, 2020

Son, I'm happy as a sea slug just watching the moon stretch &
shimmy. From under these ever-warming waves, son. Happy
watching it waver, that coin from some distant people, feeling
you grow each bone you need inside your thin membrane. Got
my brood pouch, got a current for a cradle. Here to keep you &
keep you safe, son, from my coronet to my tail tip. Here's hoping
that coin won't fall down here! My boy, I fear that'd break my
bony plates. Not sure I could regulate the salinity for you if the
moon came flipping at us. My main move is holding on—got
this tail wrapped around the seagrass, got these tiny fins. Won't
take us far, but we'll stay upright. A heart in my head, son, a
head ripe with a little heart. You're growing one too; soon you'll
be upright as me. Same toothless snout, same useless fins. I'm a
keeper, son. You'll be a keeper too. The moon shrinks, it grows.
I'll hold on right here for you. It's what we can do.

Be Enough

But when he stumbles it's
the world's betrayed him.

This belief the ground will always
be level, or rather, that stepping
forward will never require belief.

But this stool is trying to stand
with two legs termite-honeycombed.

And at the stairs he takes a step
then stops, arms up, expecting
some overseer to lift him. And I do.

This guiding our children to move
their minds like fire, like flood.

This clutching our parents against
our own sick hearts, and how
to hear their garble as song.

We sweep the path before him
and we never mind our wake.

This populous dark
inside his bedroom he finds
with some new words enkindled.

But we love the mutilated dolls,
their arm sockets, expectationless.

This ungentle touch he has
for the bodies of others,
swinging from a shopping cart.

But he names each pizza crust, a train
he carries, chock with desire.

He cries *empathy* in the bath
stacking ducks on top of ducks,
a present but not for anyone.

This buckled world we grieve and give,
as if the world will always be enough.

Mine

A pale oar leans into its dust
beside the fireplace full
of junk mail. Above, lodged
in a model boat, a rock
with a face painted on it,

a peachy rictus slapped there
by some bored kid. One sail
like a thunder sheet backstage
trails the last of its three masts,
angled toward the window,

where the sun and bugs are
active. Here's the dark corner,
here the bright socks. Plastic tiger
forgotten on the kitchen table.
Cantaloupe rind and ant poison.

These chairs must be real wicker,
they seem so expensively frail.
And garbage on the beach seems
precious. Some kids screech
and someone else loves them.

The ocean sounds pale. The sky
looks phony and far too eager.
I have something important
sleeping in the room behind me.
It's not for you, world. It's mine.

V ◆ Field Guide

Field Guide

Be the brown bear and the honeybee,
the finch and the squirrel,

both too picky for this birdseed.
Be the real train rattling

past the clenched model trains,
and be those too, damp,

printed with small-hand sweat.
Be the anglerfish with its dark

relationship to light, and be
the shadow puppet duck

who lives along the ceiling.
Be the pine needles and

keep calling them *hay*.
Be a new vowel, an open one.

In the whorls of your hair
be an impossible map, and in

following that map be
a detour into a coconut grove.

Be the lion and the whip,
the icicle and crunch of winter

grass underfoot. Be louder.
Be the rod and the spoils.

Be the bucket of hairs and
the shirt that grows and grows.

Or be a grown mule hauling
your mother and me down

a cliffside gravel path, and be
the canyon backdrop

we ignore. Be the cracked
spine and the uncut pages.

Be two rogue daisies and
the merciful gardener.

After the bath be the schooner
dry docked in a flamingo blanket,

gaff-rigged like a pirate
and slick of foot, laughing,

kicking, laughing. And after
the rains be the water strider

grown too fat to stand above
the surface tension of the puddle,

little predator, indiscriminate
feeder ours. Be the temple,

and be the apostate. Be the legs
like bamboo in their visible

growth, and be the favorite
pants, worried to comfort,

their thin knees presenting
each thread. Be the curved

slide and the mulched tires
waiting like earth at the end.

From where in your elbow
I pulled you apart, be

resilient, be the gorilla
slipping your tears quickly

into laughter, and from that
laughter be the doctor

who snaps your tendons into place.
Be all these arms, their presence

like the net around a trampoline.
Be the apple, and be yourself

eating it in the shopping cart.
Be the door with no house

around it, and be the air
slowly nudging it open.

Be the sycamore of Berryman
and the sycamore of Wells,

strangers embracing
through a mirror. Be the city

bus and the school bus.
Be the sun's difficult salutation

and our squints into it. Be
an orange rind thrown at highway

speeds from the passenger
window, glowing in the snow,

and be the orange-vested
convict stabbing it like trash.

Be the sitcom and the lonely
critic, the genuine laughter

looped to a lie. Be honest
as a kitten, and be the kitten's

unpracticed claws. Be
apricot trees and bracken,

be blackberries and bromine,
our messy, mathematical world.

Be the dried paint left like a scab
on a borrowed shirt, and be

the friend who never mentioned it.
Be the lamb and the wire's barb.

Be each brick, and be the building.
When the vase begins to crack,

be the eye that prefers it, a lover
of wobble. Be a voice for no heifer

and no priest, but the unseen town
they left behind. And be the voice

that calls that town into being.
My son, be the praise song

pushed at the impossible sky. Be
still as an old couch and be still

beside me. My son, be
forever. Be small forever.

"Grown-up Love" is for Rachel Rosenberg-Shoch. "Mine" is for Lily Brown. "For Grandma V." is also for Ryan Elsenbeck. "Be Enough" owes its empathy to Macy Smolsky. Several of these poems are part of an ongoing conversation with visual artist Kasia Ozga's mixed-media works on paper. Shilo McGiff provided invaluable insights during the editing process. Thank you, Kiki Petrosino, for reminding me of our first duty. This whole book is for Becca Myers and Miles Rosenberg, as am I.